1

Why I Back The Blue

By Guy Smilie

Why I Back The Blue - Chapter 1

Hi, My Name is Guy and I committed crimes. I spent a great deal of my childhood without a Father after my Dad died of cancer when I was in the sixth grade. Rebellion and charm were characteristic of my early life. At the same time, for the majority of my upbringing I have had the beginnings of a relationship with Jesus Christ.

Impulsivity and the ability to cry my way out of trouble were evident throughout my youth. In the first grade, I remember throwing burrs in a girl's winter hat. The consequence for my behavior was the tedious removal of all burr fragments. Yes, the tears appeared. Was this manipulation, impulsivity, or the start of mental illness? Perhaps all these elements were at play.

You may ask, "Who was Jesus to me? Why did He matter? Was I a hypocrite? Did I have a good family?"

At the age of 6, I walked up to an orange, brown sofa chair with my Mom to ask Jesus into my heart. Why do I remember this? Is this a significant aspect of my life? A seed was planted by the God of Our Universe.

Mom and Dad were determined to see this seed grow and took me to church throughout my youth. Alongside this seed, weeds grew. I was selfish and demanded attention. I almost accidentally burned down the house.

In 8th Grade, I began a Ritalin prescription for ADHD and regularly visited a psychologist. Ritalin seemed to be a wonder drug. My behavior improved greatly and I began achieving good grades in middle school. My Mom said in the early years of high school, "You could get all 4.0s if you really wanted to."

I was infuriated. Wasn't I doing good enough already? Soon, I began receiving report cards of all 4.0s. As a high schooler heavily involved in sports, music, and academic achievement, my reputation seemed invincible. Every flaw in me seemed to be overlooked by teachers.

It must have been hard for my Mom to raise me alone. Was it worthwhile for her not to give up on a child determined to paint her and anyone I did not get my 100% way with as the enemy?

I eventually moved out as I came of age, forgetting the Mother that had been instrumental in my rehabilitation from a freshman year car accident.

(I flew over the roof of a car at 40 miles per hour. The following summer my Mom and me frequented a high school track for a pivotal time of healing and training. Everything fell into place as I began to run Cross-Country, joined the

Wrestling Team, and excel.)

Despite this great history, as I moved out, I

forsook my family and glued into a computer lab

chatting online with every spare moment.

Irresponsibly I simply focused on myself. My

alienation towards authority would pinnacle with

involvement in the 1999 MSU Riots.

Why I Back The Blue - Chapter 2

Who did I answer to? What did a relationship

with God mean to me? Did I have a

conscientious? I looked out the window and saw

a thousand people assemble to take over Grand

River Avenue in East Lansing, Michigan. It was like

jumping on a roller coaster. I made my way to the

front of the crowd. My impulsivity peaked. I

joined two college gatherings that opposed the

police. I was a thrill-seeker answering to no one.

Post-Riot, I developed some guilt and turned

myself into the police. I sought attention from

media outlets. My wings would be cut soon.

When people learned of my behavior, I was pulled

out of activities that I loved. I was removed from living in a college Christian Co-Op.

Mercy was shown to me like a Father Figure by the police. I craved this! I needed direction and a role model. I would end up being convicted of the Misdemeanor Disorderly Conduct: Assembly To Riot.

My Mom would attend all the monthly probation meetings with me. My Probation Officer Matthew Brundage was always kind to me. He exemplified professionalism and respect. Years later, when I appeared before the court for the expungement process, I shared with Officer Brundage how well everything was going for me. He put in a good word for me to the judge.

As much as I was devastated losing many opportunities post-riot, I remained in the Lansing Community College Honors Program. As Adjunct Faculty, Instructor Robert R. Budd reached out to me. He was expert at research and far along in age. I needed his help to complete a persuasive writing course. Mister Budd allowed me to stretch my incomplete for 2 years as he poured out his wisdom in writing and investigative research.

Unfortunately, I still had a bad attitude in many ways. I frequently disrespected Mister Budd despite him pouring his intellect into me for the course work and investigative toy history research. Robert Budd would not give up on me. He shared his talents learned after attending Yale Graduate School.

In 2000, I created an impressive online newsletter about the toy designing firm Marvin Glass & Associates. Using the skills I learned, I found a flaw in an online article written by the inventor of the first video game system Odyssey, Ralph Baer. The inventor allowed me to interview him by phone for the newsletter and correspond with him by e-mail for a research project involving 5th Grade Students.

Why I Back the Blue - Chapter 3

What does this have to do with Back The Blue?

Why do I support law enforcement now? There

are no throwaways. Criminals will at times accept

mentoring. They are complex people with

potential. People who demonstrate tough love

and mercy make ripple effects into lives.

Jesus planted that seed in me in my childhood and

Mister Budd fearlessly poured into me

academically. Officer Brundage showed me his

example of someone in the law enforcement

system who cared when it seemed I had no one.

We may never see the results of our efforts.

Instructor Robert Budd and Officer Brundage have

since passed away leaving great legacies. Looking

back I see many setbacks in my life, but I am glad

who I am becoming today. Do not give up on your

investment in others. Plant a seed. Invest in

those who have no one.

Never stop learning; "Making the most of every opportunity for the days are evil (Ephesians 5:16)." Many times medicine is necessary. We must learn not to label people or systems as 100% good or 100% evil. We need to give others the room to improve and not place complete trust in the imperfect. Multiple people have come up to me and told me God is going to heal me. They claim with their doctrine that I will not need meds anymore.

Ultimately, I live with the decision to abruptly stop medicine if I follow what some people say. Repeatedly I have been hospitalized and put on court-order to take medication. Some people

make blanket statements that psychiatry is

completely corrupt.

I learn to stop judging with 100% blanket

conclusions. I use this investigative lens to come

to conclusions about my faith, mental health, and

law enforcement.

As a freshman in college, my guide was the flawed wisdom of my peers. They chose to interpret authority as people to be disregarded. The newspaper reported on rebellious young adults inciting civil disturbances. I went with the flow.

As you decide where you stand in the support or rebellion towards authority, consider that no one is perfect except God who instructs us to submit. We all error—even those we look up to. Let's give others the benefit of the doubt, but let's not set up ourselves to be victims.

I have been assaulted by individuals who were probably abusing drugs and/or alcohol. The stitches I received to my face and punch to my temple taught me to be careful about who I let into my circle. No matter what happens, we cannot stop being grateful.

Praise the Lord I have a place to live. Praise God I have daily food. Praise God for family and friends. Life is a mixture of not completely good and not completely bad.

Why I Back The Blue - Chapter 6

Who in their right mind would desire captivity?

Who would with freedom, food, and friendship

desire to be incarcerated or hospitalized? This has

been my interest for the purpose of independent

investigative journalism. (I have let leaders know

about this desire.)

Attempting social experiments: walking through

my city in a hospital gown and a fake jail jumpsuit.

I have tested the boundaries in the jumpsuit on

the Capitol Steps, in the police station, and inside

an FBI building. Somehow, authorities have just

let me be. A law enforcement leader I respect

returned my e-mail.

His professionalism and friendship touched my heart. I threw that jumpsuit in the trash. How do we win over those on the wrong path? The answer is genuine friendship and respect.

For years, professional relationships have been
nurtured between Community Mental Health
Workers and myself. Many case managers
experienced high-turnover during this time, but
they have all definitely cared about me. They
have endured appointments with me resisting
medication—just listening to me talk about the
adventures I go on. At CMHA-CEI, professionalism
is maintained, but the door is open for creativity
in therapy. I thank Jesus for them—even when
they have been incredibly different than me.

These professionals follow person-centered
planning as a model. Meetings are largely about

my experiences. I am given the opportunity to set my own goals and be supported. An important element of reaching out to consumers is having them regularly check in by their own volition. Thank you Jesus for those who have built long-term relationships with me—God, my Mom, Mister Budd, Community Mental Health Authority of Clinton, Eaton, and Ingham Counties, and law enforcement.

The best practice to deal with a rebel is not to get rid of him/her, but to win him/her over. Surprise the person. Bust his/her paradigms wide open. Persuade the person want to share his/her talents in the midst of imperfection.

When a leader reaches out to people that may

otherwise be marginalized, there is societal

transformation. Yes Lord! I may not see eye to

eye with the political views of the Former 12 Year

Mayor of the Capitol City Lansing, Michigan, but I

cannot deny that he continually cares enough to

show me personal attention. When Former

Mayor Virg Bernero was in office, I arranged for

him to conduct an open forum at Justice In Mental

Health Organization Drop-In with consumers who

struggle with issues such as homelessness,

substance abuse issues, breaking the law, and

mental illness.

Former Mayor Virg Bernero saw value in the

Common People as he has seen mental illness in

his own family. I believe that little is accomplished by using valuable time whining to our clones. The secret is being brave enough to have coffee with those different than us. How can we win over people who may be mistaken without fear?

"For God did not give us a spirit of fear, but of power, of love, and of a sound mind (1 Timothy 1:7)." We have been made special and are called to greatness. Let's meet those who we do not understand.

Why I Back The Blue - Chapter 8

Christmas was special this year. I did my normal State Capitol walk and noticed there was a yule goat placed on the lawn by the West Michigan Satanic Temple.

The reality that there was no Nativity in sight disturbed me. Remember, the 100% Rule? I didn't follow it. I viewed the makers of the goat as dark, dangerous, and unreachable. I wrote on Facebook, "I wish someone would trash it." I proceeded to set up my own Nativity on the Capitol lawn without a permit. The Michigan State Capitol Facility Operations reached out to me on Facebook Messenger about getting registered.

Thank God what great mercy I was shown. I began to interact with Satanists on social media. I learned that they can be friendly and religiously pluralistic. The 100% Judgment was my error. I could not label those who I do not understand, but need to meet them to discover the truth. To come to this conclusion I recall all those who invested in me morally, spiritually, and with the hand of friendship over time.

Where am I today and how can we help law enforcement? Take the time to get to know them. Fear not. Walk into the police department even when there is no urgency. Attend City, Police Commissioner, Mental Health, and other leadership meetings. Become educated about important issues such as disease, elder abuse, human trafficking, mental health, diversity—whatever you have a heart for or need a heart for.

January 12th, 2018, save the date. I attended a "Human Trafficking Seminars" Training and invited two people to come with me. What a tear-jerker. I was clueless to the reality that this evil was prevalent close to home. The seminar shook me to my core. I bawled and would never be the same again.

You are reading my book; take the time to do something! Become educated. Pray for the hurting. Meet a need.

The Human Trafficking Seminar blew me away when I learned the instructor had witnessed extreme abuse perpetrated by someone close to her. She did not stop there and be debilitated. She took action in educating and creating a program to help victims. This resonated with my heart forever—learning about children locked up in basements with duct tape over their mouth by even a Mom or Dad. Families were and are

betraying their own. Lord I pray.

This issue is beyond any individual by themselves:

"The United States is the number one consumer

of sex worldwide. So we are driving the demand

as a society (Geoff Rogers, co-founder of the

United States Institute Against Human

Trafficking)." We claim to be this great Christian

Nation. Should we shut down or be prompted to

action?

Thank you Jesus for your Holy Spirit. Thank you

for placing your heart in others to stand against

extreme injustice. We repent for our part in it.

Learn. Read a book. Take a class. Apply the knowledge learned.

Why I Back The Blue - Chapter 10

I learned from job about mandated reporting. It was my duty to recognize suspected child abuse and document it. In Lansing, even if you are poor without a phone, you can walk into the police department, pick up the red phone, and make a difference. For urgencies you may call 911. With less urgency, you can contact Non-Emergency Ingham County Dispatch. I am in favor of this public service.

In Lansing, pick up your cell phone and call 517-483-4600 ext. 2 for Non-Emergency needs in the community. An old man or woman may be in great pain. A young person may potentially be in danger and need a welfare check. When I call them they typically respond on the phone within two minutes and send an ambulance in less than five minutes.

I respect law enforcement after they respected me even in my mess. I tested them and they assured me that they have a job to do. Law Enforcement stand up for the weak as well as the seemingly strong. Police show mercy the majority of the time.

There is a growing movement called Crisis Intervention Team (CIT) and Mental Health First-Aid USA (MHFA USA). CIT is an international model to teach police de-escalation in mental health emergencies. They do an excellent job. Police in Lansing are accommodating to people with diverse needs. They take the time to consider mental health and deserve our respect.

Yes we do live in a fallen world. There are people who are corrupt in different positions in society, but how better to influence this system than to talk to leaders within? Former Lansing Police Department Chief Michael Yankowski spoke eloquently at the C.O.P.S. Memorial in the Michigan State Capitol Rotunda:

"Greater love has no man than this that he lay down his life for his friend (John 15:13)." This quote comes from the Bible and points out that police take a vow to serve us to the death. Thank you Jesus for the police.

Back to Human Trafficking... What do we do if we witness someone being exploited? We step in and report to the authorities. Before I understood the process, I was hanging out with a friend who almost became trafficked. A stranger in the park gave her alcohol and tried to win her over. I knew I had to follow them. At a table under a bridge, he tried to coerce her to consume cocaine in her nose. I stood my ground as he told her that he wanted to take her out of the state. The man offered me $50 to abandon her. I replied, "If she takes the cocaine by choice, I am leaving, but if she does not want it, I am not leaving."

I put my hand on a Bible and said, "You can take out a gun and shoot me, I am not leaving." Somehow the atmosphere shifted at that moment. The two men sitting there, my friend, and me joined hands in prayer. She was released and God had done a miracle. My friend told me that she secretly had put her hand on the Bible. As she spoke, she was shaking like me, but God had rescued us!

If this trafficking situation had occurred today, I would have contacted the authorities. Now I would call local police, the FBI, and the National Trafficking Hotline. The Human Trafficking Seminar had taught me how to communicate with diverse leaders in safety who can recognize a pattern and do something about it. Reporting to all applicable agencies about Human Trafficking is not a mistake. It is making sure that everyone possible is aware to best address gross, organized criminal corruption.

Be calm and clear on the phone. Where is the danger located even it is just suspected? What are the facts? What are the ages of the people involved? What time did the danger arise?

I am blessed that I used to work for the National Passport Information Center (U.S. Department of State, Peckham). I learned that it takes a whole team of ordinary people like you and me to represent the government.

I once had a friend who was a victim of online exploitation. A predator had asked for her to show inappropriate pictures of herself and threatened to expose her if she didn't show more. I read her chatlogs and went to his Facebook page. I discovered that this man belonged to underage dating groups. My suspicion was that the predator was doing this to many young people and was part of a ring.

It was December 24, 2018, 2:00am and FBI Lansing was closed. I decided to call FBI Washington, D.C. Office in case a crime ring was involved. FBI asked me for my full name, Date of

Birth, and Address. FBI took my report seriously to the point of forwarding my report to FBI Detroit and instructing me to fill out a IC3.gov FBI Internet Crime Report.

I did not stop there. I called the National Trafficking Hotline to make sure I had covered all the bases. The Hotline documented my report for future reference and compassionately treated me with dignity. Thank you God for those who fearlessly serve us 24/7/365.

Is there room for corruption? Yes. That is why we inform more than one agency of the dangers we witness in Human Trafficking. For the most part, I trust those who protect us. We live in an imperfect world and our voice matters. Multiple points of view and testimonies matter.

Remember to contact Internal Affairs if you witness corruption. Do not be a vigilante, but rather report to those who can advocate.

During my stay at a mental hospital, I witnessed a psychiatric technician body slamming a patient. Alone my testimony might have seemed like an isolated product of mental illness, but I was not the only one reporting to Recipient Rights (I did not know this at the time.). The Nurse Manager appeared in my room with a typed piece of paper indicating that action had been taken after my report.

Wow. I was empowered. Even as a patient I had a voice to protect others and so do you!

Why I Back The Blue - Chapter 15

Everyone can make a difference; I am on disability. I do not drive or work except for my service in two consumer advisory councils. I take psychotropic medication, but just like you I have a voice to make this world a better place.

I have chosen to dress in Thin Blue Line clothing almost every day. It's my way of saying I support law enforcement. I speak at Lansing police commissioner meetings and other leadership meetings. We do not have to wait until we have obvious power to make a difference. Recently, there was a 9/11 Monument on a marble base in Wentworth Park, Lansing, Michigan, USA that had its inscription wearing away. I took a picture by the suggestion of a friend and the City of Lansing promptly fixed it.

In my community there is a Lansing Police Department phone app. Anyone can make an anonymous or non-anonymous tip at any time from their phone. We can help officers by reaching out. We are the Checks and Balances. This is Beautiful America. If you have a position in society, use it to make a difference. If you are disabled, use your free time to communicate your perspective. I have a voice and time while I am on disability to invest. If you wish you had a phone application like the LPD App in your area, download the Crime Stoppers App called, "P3."

The app covers regions all over the United States.

Send in a tip. Invest in those who cannot repay.

Make a dent.

Why I Back The Blue - Chapter 16

In proactively learning, start local. Mobilize others. Submit an article. Speak at a conference. We all have a voice and can listen. Chief Daryl Green of Lansing Police Department listens and acts. As consumers, my friends and I have had the opportunity to share our perspective with someone who cares a great deal.

If you are in a position of power or if you just want someone to listen to your perspective do not neglect communicating/learning. As a result of my reporting, the entrance to Lansing Police Department Headquarters now has an improved brochure box that includes quite a few Human

Trafficking Hotline Information Sheets.

Why I Back The Blue – Chapter 17

Reporting Contacts

Urgent Life and Death Emergencies – 911

Ingham County Non-Emergency Dispatch

1-517-483-4600 ext. 2

Crime Stoppers Phone App – P3

Lansing Police Department Phone App – Tips &

More!

FBI Internet Crime Reporting – http://ic3.gov

FBI Lansing – 1- 517-336-8367

FBI Detroit – 1-313-965-2323

FBI Washington, D.C. – 1-202-324-3000

Child Protective Services Central Intake (CPS) –

1-855-444-3911

CMHA-CEI Crisis Services (Mental Health) –

 1-517-346-8460

East Lansing Non-Emergency Police –

1-517-351-4220

Lansing Township Non-Emergency Police –

1-517-485-1700

Lansing Police Department Internal Affairs –

1-517-483-4804

Michigan State University Non-Emergency Police –

1-517-355-2221

National Child Abuse Hotline – 1-800-422-4453

National Domestic Abuse Hotline –

 1-800-799-7233

National Human Trafficking Hotline –

1-888-373-7888

National Suicide Hotline – 1-800-273-8255

U.S. Secret Service (Threats On President) –

 1-202-406-5708

Why I Back The Blue - Chapter 18

Where am I today? Did that seed that God planted at the sofa chair make a difference? Yes and God has made it grow. I have learned to confess that Jesus is Lord of all and believe that he was raised from the dead. Jesus is my hero even when I do not measure up. The world is not 100% reliable. He can change anyone—including those I have despised. He hasn't given up on me in all of my mess. God has changed lives of many people in even corruption.

"Repent and be baptized, every one of you, in the name of Jesus, for the remission of sin and you shall receive the gift of the Holy Ghost, (Acts 2:38-40)."

Repentance is a 180 degree turn from evil. It is a confession of our sins to God and a new start every time we have compromised through wrong action. "If we confess our sins he is faithful and just to forgive our sins and to cleanse us from all unrighteousness (1 John 1:9)."

We are not perfect, but if we commit to God, we are seen as perfect because of Jesus's sacrifice on the cross.

"But he was wounded for our transgressions, he was bruised for our iniquities, the chastisement of our peace was upon him; and with his stripes we are healed (Isaiah 53:5)."

What is healing? No person has a perfect human body. I believe healing is the conversion to our best self. We are not accidents and we do sin, but God has a world of opportunity for us. We can enjoy making this world a better place.

When I "Back The Blue," I am saying I may not be perfect, but I am here for you. I appreciate the commitment of law enforcement. I thank you for being patient with me. I want to be like you and be willing to lay down my life for others. I have seen dedication in officers who have reached out to me. I have seen the power of Jesus in the lives